FOR SUCH A TIME AS THIS

Answering the Call to Live a
Life of Purpose and Obedience

Crystal Daye

Forward by Clerol Austrie

Copyright © 2017. Crystal Daye. All Rights Reserved.

Empowered for Such a Time as This.

Printed in the United States of America.

No portion of this book may be reproduced, stored in a retrieval system, or transmitted in any form or by any means except for brief quotations in printed reviews without the prior written permission of Crystal Daye and DayeLight Publishers Limited.

Unless otherwise indicated, all scripture quotations are taken from the Holy Bible, American Standard Version and King James (American Version).

For information regarding special discounts for bulk purchase, please contact DayeLight Publishers Limited at dayelightinternationalja@gmail.com

Book Cover Design by ArcJack Designs

ISBN: 978-0-9994025-6-6

ACKNOWLEDGEMENT

My Abba Father in Heaven, thank You for entrusting me with the privilege, passion, and gift to write this book. Thank You for using me as a chosen vessel to represent You. All my praise and worship belong to You Lord.

To my amazing and supportive family, I love you, to the core of my being. Thank you for believing in me.

All my mentors, social media family, friends, supporters, well-wishers, customers, clients, sisters and brothers in faith, thank you for the prayers, encouragement, laughter, and support. I love you!

To my editors, proof-readers, graphic designers and the rest of the team that helped to bring this book to life, I am grateful for your assistance.

I pray that God will continue to bless you all!

DEDICATION

This book is dedicated to all the women who believe that they are destined for greatness. You know you don't deserve God's blessing, but you are so grateful for His love, mercy, and grace.

This book is for the women who are sick and tired of settling for less than God's best. You know you have a story, you have a purpose, and you desire to use your talents or gifts to impact others.

This book is for the mothers, sisters, aunts, grandmothers, and daughters that have experienced challenges and hardships that should have killed them, BUT GOD! You made it through, not one storm, but through many, and even the one you're going through now, Sis, you will make it!

So if you consider yourself a purpose-driven woman, ambitious woman, a woman of faith, kingdom woman or godly woman, this book was written for you! Arise Daughters of Zion; you are ***Empowered for Such a Time as This***!!

PREFACE

I wrote this book in a season where many times I did not feel successful. I had just turned 30 years old and I had my own definition of what "success" should look like.

Yes, I am a Christian woman who loves Jesus, but I had dreams. I dreamt of being debt-free; that my child could attend a nice private school and that I could afford nice vacations with my family. I envisioned being at the peak of my career; completing my Master's Degree, serving in ministries at church and yes, probably being courted by the love of my life.

Of course, this was all possible for me but, was it my plan or His?

"Many are the plans in a person's heart, but it is the LORD's purpose that prevails."

– ***Proverbs 19:21***

Instead, I found myself in a season where God started to show me what real success is—a life of obedience, surrender, purpose, and faith in Him!

I took the most significant leap of faith and left my full-time job on January 20, 2017, in obedience to God. I left without a plan, but I had a promise; His promise. The Lord told me I would be a full-time minister and entrepreneur. I had snippets of what I should be doing, but honestly, it didn't make much sense to me because I wasn't sure what the total picture should look like. I could not picture what He wanted for me.

Everything in my life started to look like the opposite of success. I had no job, which means no source of consistent income. I moved back to my mother's house, a place I vowed never to return. I was in debt above my head which sunk me into depression. There was no sign of a husband, I dropped out of my Master's Degree programme, and the business that God had promised me didn't look so promising at all.

The ministry and Church home I loved, the people I called family for over seven years, God told me the season was over, and I had to leave.

In that season I had so many emotions running through me. I felt:

- Clueless like Abraham *(**Genesis 12:1**)*, when God told him to leave to an unknown land.

- Abandoned like Job *(**Job 1:13-22**)*, when He lost everything even though he was faithful to God.

- Bitter like Naomi (***Ruth 1:20***), when she felt that God had forsaken her.

But it was in that season my faith was challenged to believe God's promises over my feelings. In the many moments, I felt faithless, abandoned or depressed; I had to trust God's Word.

> *"God will never abandon the faithful or ever give help to evil people. He will let you laugh and shout again."*
>
> *– Job 8: 20-21*

I saw success differently. It looked "foolish" to the common man, but I became confident in knowing that I was driven by His plans. This success was birth from surrender, despite the world telling me to "have it my way." It was through obedience and faith that I was reminded that I am empowered for such a time as this!

TABLE OF CONTENTS

Forward by Clerol Austrie 1
Sending You Gratitude 3
Introduction 5
How to Use This Book 7
Empowerment Prayer 11

Chapter 1: Are You Hot or Cold? 13
    Are You Hot or Cold? 14

Chapter 2: Called for Such a Time as This 23
    1 – Called To Salvation 24
    2 – Called To Identity 26
    3 – Called To Purpose 27
    So, how do you answer the call? 29

Chapter 3: Becoming an Empowered Woman 33
    What is Empowerment? 34
    Who is a Godly Empowered Woman? 35
    Why are you Empowered for Such a Time as This?.. 35
    Here are Eight Practical Tips on
    Becoming an Empowered Woman 38

Chapter 4: Got Idols? 55

Chapter 5: Courage to Obey 63
    It takes courage to be obedient to God 65

Chapter 6: Positioned for Purpose 69
    What is the meaning of "Purpose"? 70
    Being In Position Is Key! 72
    Our Purpose Is In Christ 73

Our Purpose Is Becoming All God
Has Called Us To Be 73
Purpose Is Not About You.. 75
Where You Are Now, You Are Positioned............... 75
What A Mighty And Faithful God We Serve 76
Be Careful That Your Dream Don't
Become An Idol 77

Chapter 7: Defining Success God's way 81
Success Begins With Receiving God's
Gift Of Salvation 84
Seek Excellence, Not Success 86
Vivian Jokotade's 3 Recipe For Success 86

Chapter 8: Turning Your Mess into A Message 91

Chapter 9: Truth About Self-love 107

Chapter 10: Empowered Woman Resource Guide 113
Daily Habits Of An Empowered Woman............... 114
Inspirational Quotes For The
Empowered Woman.. 116
Self-Reflection Journal Questions
For The Empowered Woman 118
10 Scriptures For Empowered Woman................... 123
31- Day Biblical Declarations For
An Empowered Woman.. 124

Letter to Royalties: A Surrendered Life......................... 129
For Such A Time As This is
investing in today 130

Conclusion 131

About the Author 133

FORWARD

It is time; it is your time to rise, to be present, to show up and do what you were created for. You and your purpose have been in the making long before now. God told Jeremiah, *"I formed you in the womb, I knew you, before you were born I set you apart." (Jeremiah 1:6).*

God appointed you before you physically existed, and you are here at this time because you were created for a time such as this. This book will guide you in seeking God, in learning what you were created and called for and push you to stop all hesitation. Your purpose was in existence before you, and God created you for it and He made no mistake.

Do not allow the devil to get in the way of this by entertaining thoughts of doubts, fear of incompetence, fear of not being good enough, fear of not knowing enough, and not being popular enough. God just needs you to be available. It's His show; you just need to be wholeheartedly present.

God told Jeremiah *"Do not say that you are too young" (Jeremiah 1:7),* so you shouldn't say that you are not good enough, or any other excuse you may have. God went on to say, *"everywhere I send you, you will go, all that I command you, you shall speak."*

My sister, do what God wants you to do, say what God wants you to say, and you will reach the people you were meant to reach.

Clerol Austrie

SENDING YOU GRATITUDE

Thank You so much for buying this book. As an expression of my gratitude, I would like to offer you a "*7 Day Affirmation Cards for Kingdom Women.*" To download for FREE, please visit: www.crystaldaye.com/freebies

INTRODUCTION

Have you ever felt that there was so much more potential within you that you haven't tapped into yet?

Do you look around you and it seems like everybody is doing the things you wish you were doing?

How many conversations have God had with you where He told you that He has a bigger plan for you than what you are currently settling for?

I know settling into your comfort zone is easier. Even though you secretly have the desire (that God placed within you) to do more and be more, you wonder who are you, to deserve to be doing that.

This book is not about you achieving success how the world defines it. There are many who have achieved wealth, expensive vehicles, beautiful marriages with kids, high educational attainment, but they know they are made for more.

I come to provoke you and make you very uncomfortable. As you read this book, you will feel convicted and forced to throw this book away because it will feel like God is speaking loudly to you and it might make you feel unsettled. But I pray you will read with a repentant heart.

Everywhere I go to minister, I meet women who have so much purpose in them, but fear and disobedience have often held them back. Many of us are so busy looking at what others are doing; we often do not realize that God wants to use us to do something too.

This life is not about you. Your story or message is not about you. Your gifts and talents are not about you. Your obedience and purpose are so much bigger than you. You are placed on this earth to make an impact. Whether to 10 persons or 10,000 persons, your contribution in life is necessary.

Yes, it might mean that it is time for you to start that blog, write that book, start that business, go back to school, apply for that job, go on that mission trip, adopt that child, intercede more for your family, speak out, sing that song, say that poem, address that situation, post that status, forgive that person, give "that" away, sow that money, reconcile that friendship, let go of that relationship, join that ministry, or launch that organization. I don't know what it is that God will have you do by the end of this book. But my sister, God wants me to remind you that **YOU ARE EMPOWERED FOR SUCH A TIME AS THIS!**

HOW TO USE THIS BOOK

Many times we read books and it makes us feel good, but we put it on a shelf and never look at it again. *This is not one of those books!*

This book is not just for reading, but it is for working. Yes, it will require you to do some (maybe a lot) of journaling, search the scriptures and be vulnerable in order for you to be transformed. It is a book you will keep very close to you, whether in the car, on your bedside table or your office desk – this way you can reach for it anytime you need affirmation or encouragement about God's divine purpose for your life.

Each chapter has journal reflection questions, practical suggestions and steps to help you in your journey of self-discovery. You will need to pause, be still and listen to what God is saying to you about a particular topic.

Of course, you will need to be in fervent prayer because we know the enemy does not want you to walk in the fullness of your potential.

It will be helpful to get an accountability partner. Suggest it to your youth and women's group, book club or encourage friends to get their own copy.

Commit to the use of this book.

Remember knowledge is not power. APPLIED knowledge is power.

So prepare to act!

Royalty, I am praying for you.

I love you. God loves you more!

Your sister in Christ,

Crystal Daye

GOD'S GOT YOU.

LET'S BEGIN!!

EMPOWERMENT PRAYER

Dear God, I come humbly before You as Your daughter surrendering my all to You. Lord, who am I that You are mindful of me? I'm just a sinner saved by Your grace who desires more than anything else to please You with my whole life. Father forgive me for the times I didn't put You first. Forgive me for the idols I placed before You and for all the times I allowed sin to creep into my heart and plague my life. Forgive me Lord even as I forgive others.

Lord thank You so much for the gifts, talents, passions and knowledge you have blessed me with. I thank You for choosing me to fulfil Your purpose on this earth so I can contribute to the expansion of Your kingdom and be a blessing to others.

Father, I am truly grateful that I am Your daughter and that I can come boldly before You because of what Your Son, Jesus Christ did for me on the Cross. Oh Lord, thank You for that unconditional love, enduring mercy and unexplainable favour You have bestowed upon me.

Jesus, I love You with my whole heart and I'm sold out for You! My desire is to please You with my life and at the end of my journey to hear, "well done my good and faithful servant." In Your name, I pray Amen!

Chapter 1

ARE YOU HOT OR COLD?

On January 1, 2014, my life shifted. I believe it was that early morning that I **answered the call of God** on my life.

I stood in *Absinthe*, a New Year's Eve party, trying to enjoy my last party with my friends but honestly, I felt out of place. Sitting there, I no longer found the music entertaining or the liquor appealing instead I wished I was at church. I loved my friends and wanted to enjoy the time with them, but inside I was battling with the decision to walk away from the life I was living.

No one understood it, but I knew with all my heart serving GOD wholeheartedly was my true desire and I was ready to forsake it all to follow Jesus Christ.

Are You Hot or Cold?

For months, I was experiencing an internal battle of wanting to surrender my life and live for Christ; but I was too afraid to do it. I got baptized in December 2009, and I was going to church, doing devotions and praying to God, but I was living a lukewarm life.

> *"I know your deeds; you are neither cold nor hot. How I wish you were one or the other. So because you are lukewarm — neither hot nor cold — I am about to spit you out of My mouth!"*
>
> **– *Revelations 3:15-16***

Living lukewarm meant I was saying all the "churchly" things, but I wasn't living a life pleasing to God. Instead, I was clubbing, gossiping, fornicating, cursing, dressing skimpily and not living my full potential in Christ. Even though I was saying I had a relationship with God, there was no fruit of this being shown.

Now, you may ask, "Crystal, but how does living lukewarm relate to answering the call on my life?" Let me tell you that living out your calling or fulfilling your purpose makes no sense if you don't choose to live a life of obedience to God. Being lukewarm means, you say you follow Jesus, but really in your heart you don't, so your actions and heart for God are not in sync.

If you were not a woman who desires to live for God, you wouldn't have picked up this book. I know if you didn't desire to live a life of purpose, obedience, faith, surrender and walk in God's full potential, then you would not be reading this book. So it is my greatest desire that you understand the foundation of being a godly empowered woman.

As the scripture states, God hates someone who lives in a lukewarm state. God would prefer that we be either hot or cold, because being lukewarm is seriously dangerous. It's dangerous because you think everything is fine and that you are in right relationship with God but He is ready to spit you out.

Let's start with some self-reflection. Here are five ways to evaluate if you are lukewarm:

1. You don't want to give up sin; you simply want to be saved from the penalty of sin.

Many times, we get baptized and go to church because we believe it will save us from going to hell. We haven't truly repented (hate sin and turn away from it and turn to Christ), instead, we are remorseful when we do certain "bad" deeds, but we aren't willing to give up our old life and walk in a new life in Christ.

– 2 Corinthians 5:17, 1 John 3:6

Personal Reflection

What does your relationship with sin look like? Do you make excuses that you are imperfect, which is why you sin, or do you repent when you're convicted of sin?

_____

_____

_____

_____

_____

_____

_____

_____

Chapter 1: Are You Hot or Cold?

Personal Prayer

Write a brief prayer to God about sin and its impact on your life, and your desire for Him to help you in your walk.

_____
_____
_____
_____
_____
_____
_____
_____
_____

2. **People around you don't take your walk with Christ seriously.**

    I know for me, I used to be the one my friends would call on to pray for them, and if I invite them to church, they would come. But I couldn't minister to them because they were aware of the sinful life I was living. Yes, they felt I was a little ahead because I attended church regularly, I participated in faith-based activities, and I was quick to speak about God, but I was no true example of what living for God looked like. Once I made the radical change to surrender to Him, they saw me differently. Many of them would commend me and even defend me behind my back because they saw a different person, one whose actions finally started to reflect a godly life.

If you want to know whether or not your friends take your walk with God seriously, here is how you find out. Do the usual group meet-ups, but observe the demeanor of your friends and listen to the conversations. If they become uncomfortable to have certain discussions with you or around you, ones they would usually have before you became saved, that's how you know. It is not that they think you are better than them, but they have now acknowledged that you are at a different level in your walk, in your life and they are trying to give you the respect you deserve.

(Luke 14:34-35)

Personal Reflection

How do your friends view you? Do they take your relationship with God seriously?

_____

_____

_____

_____

_____

_____

_____

3. You have not accepted that Jesus is Lord over your life.

Accepting Jesus Christ as our Savior is the easy part. Why? We all know that we are sinners in the sight of God. We know that many of the choices we make daily are led by our selfish and sinful desires, and we know we cannot save ourselves.

Here's where the challenge comes in — ***Accepting JESUS as LORD over our life.***

Get this, whether we admit it or accept it, Jesus Christ is Lord!

The problem is, we are called to surrender to His Lordship, and that's where the issue comes in. We naturally believe we know what's best for us. And many of us have the twisted idea that when we "surrender," God is going to tell us to stop doing the things dearest to us and leave the places we think we belong.

Therefore having a personal relationship with GOD is needed. The more we get to know Him intimately, the more we learn to TRUST Him. The more we trust Him, the easier SURRENDER becomes. When we know and accept that He is the GREATEST Father, we know that whatever we lose for Him cannot be compared to what He has in store for us.

(Luke 9:57-62)

Personal Reflection

Do you trust God to lead your life? What does it look like for you to allow Jesus to be your LORD?

_____

_____

_____

_____

_____

_____

_____

_____

4. You say you love others but not as much as you love yourself.

The true test of loving or serving others, is when you can give without expecting anything in return. It is giving freely and openly without seeking any form of recognition or praise. So, yes, we love our family, close friends and persons in our current circle, but little is left to love the poor, less fortunate or even our enemies. When it comes to serving or giving, we give enough so we don't feel guilty, which is the bare minimum, but our motives are self-seeking and our love is conditional.

(Luke 14:12-14)

Personal Reflection

How do you show your love for others? Do you serve or give with expectation of return?

_____

_____

_____

_____

_____

_____

You make decisions based on life on this earth more than you think about living for eternity:

Understand, we live on this earth, so we must take responsibility for ourselves so that we can survive on earth. This means eating, drinking, sleeping, working, saving, having goals and planning for a future for ourselves and our family. But, this cannot be the driving force of our lives.

One cannot be so preoccupied with storing up earthly treasures (***Matthew 6:19-21***) and seeking all the *"other"* things while forsaking their kingdom mandate (***Matthew 6:33***). You must find the balance of *loving the world* versus *living in the world*.

Personal Reflection

Do you make decisions based on eternity? Do you choose short-term pleasures over long-term gains?

_____

_____

_____

_____

_____

_____

_____

_____

Chapter 2

CALLED FOR SUCH A TIME AS THIS

Your calling is considered the customized life purpose God has ordained for you to accomplish to bring Him glory and maximize the expansion of His Kingdom.

Your call is bigger than you and customized for you.

"We are simply God's servants... Each one of us does the work which the Lord gave him to do"

- 1 Corinthians 3:5

I break down calling into three stages:

1 – CALLED TO SALVATION

Many people have heard the term '*salvation*' and you're probably not sure what it is.

According to *gotquestion.com*, salvation is *"The deliverance, by the grace of God, from eternal punishment for sin which is granted to those who accept by faith God's conditions of repentance and faith in the Lord Jesus."*

Salvation is available in Jesus alone (***John 14:6; Acts 4:12***) and is dependent on God alone for provision, assurance, and security.

Understand, this is the most important stage of your calling and the first step, even before you know who you are (identity) or what you have been called to do (purpose).

If you haven't accepted Jesus Christ as your personal Lord and Savior, then you will never be able to be a true godly *empowered* woman.

If you would like to have a relationship with God, the first step is to acknowledge that we have all sinned and that there is nothing we can do to earn God's love (**Romans 3:23-28**). We must then believe and confess that Jesus is Lord (**Romans 10:9**) and allow Him to guide our lives.

If you would like to accept Jesus as Lord of your life, you can pray the following prayer with me:

> *"Lord, I confess that I have sinned against You and ask You to forgive me. I am sorry that my sins have hurt You and other people in my life. I acknowledge that I could never earn salvation by my good works, but I come to You and trust in what Jesus did for me on the cross. I believe that You love me and that Jesus died and rose again so that I can be forgiven and come to know You. I ask You to come into my heart and be Lord of my life. I trust You with everything, and I thank You for loving me so much that I can know You here on earth and spend the rest of eternity with You in heaven. In Jesus name, Amen."*

2 – CALLED TO IDENTITY

Through accepting God's gift of salvation, we have the calling of identity. Our new identity changes our relationship with God because we can now call Him, 'Abba Father.' We can now confidently approach the King because we are now His daughters (***Romans 8:15-16***). This identity should change how we see ourselves; how we see the world and even more importantly, how the world sees us.

Our Eternal Father is a King, and we are heirs of His kingdom. We have an inheritance of royalty as daughters of the King, chosen by Him and loved dearly. We have been adopted into a kingdom with an unlimited source of power, provision, and freedom. We didn't earn this status as royalty. God chose us. Jesus signed a legal adoption through His blood. It is because of God's grace that we have been accepted with full legal status in the kingdom of God.

Knowing our identity is vital because the enemy will attack us based on our past. He will tell you that you are not worthy to do anything for God because of the sins you have committed. The enemy's job is to kill, steal and destroy your identity

(John 10:10).

Once you start questioning who you are, then feelings of inadequacy will slowly creep in and cripple you from fulfilling your purpose.

Don't skip this stage of the calling. Spend time in God's Word to find out what He has said about you; what He has promised you and what you will be rewarded with.

3 – CALLED TO PURPOSE

Purpose is the reason for existence. It is God's plan for our lives. Without purpose, life has no meaning. True success is found in acknowledging and fulfilling God's purpose for our lives (***Acts 13:36***).

> *"God has placed a specific call on your life. It may be to the marketplace, to ministry, to engineering (mine wasn't), to parenthood, to government, to the arts, and beyond— but never doubt that God created you on purpose for a purpose. He made you to play a vital role in building and advancing His kingdom."*
>
> **– John Bevere**

(**Message**)

"I glorified you on earth by completing **down to the last detail** *what you* **assigned me** *to do."*

– John 17:4

In her teaching called "*Your Call is Calling,*" Terri Savelle share these truths:

- Don't let your past keep you from answering the call.
- Don't let other people keep you from answering the call.
- Don't let finances keep you from answering the call.
- Don't let past failures keep you from answering the call.
- Don't let Satan talk you out of answering the call.
- Don't let "busy-ness" keep you from answering the call.
- Don't let shame and guilt keep you from answering the call.
- Don't let insecurity keep you from answering the call.

The Power of the Holy Spirit is essential for us to accomplish the assignment God has for our life. God will empower you to not just know His will for your life but to walk in His power to accomplish all He has called you to do and be. With this understanding, you realize we are CALLED for a purpose and God has a unique assignment for our lives. Know that your life is precious and now is the time to ANSWER God's call on your life.

Sometimes we get super enthused or even discouraged when we think about our life's purpose or calling. We wonder if we should be a Pastor or something involved with serving in the church. One of the things I've learned, on my journey, is that in different seasons we can be called to do different things. For example, long before David became King, he was a shepherd. In that season when he was taking care of the sheep, he developed skills that helped him achieve his purpose in the future season where he reigned as king of Israel, God's chosen people.

Start serving in this current season. Serve others. Use your gifts and pursue your passions.

Even your occupation can be a part of your calling. So, as a teacher, police officer, author, singer, dancer, janitor, you can be fulfilling your calling.

One thing you should never forget, your purpose will and must GLORIFY GOD. All in all, be sensitive to the Holy Spirit as He leads you on the path, towards your calling.

So, how do you answer the call?

- *Accept the gift of salvation.*

    Know that Jesus came and died for your sins, to reconcile you back to the Father. Our sin has separated us from God, and the consequence of sin is death (**Romans 6:23**). So, without having a relationship with God, you won't be able to know your calling.

- ***Surrender your plans to God.***

  Your calling is God's calling, so you can't find it without God. So give your plans to Him and He will lead you.

  "Many are the plans in a man's heart but the Lord's purpose will prevail"

  – ***Proverbs 19:21***

- ***Be open to His direction.***

  Seek to stay open to God's leading. He may lead you in ways that might surprise you.

  "Trust in the Lord with all your heart and lean not on your own understanding."

  – ***Proverbs 3:5***

- ***Believe that God wants to use you.***

  Know that your past, your finances, failures, mistakes, insecurities or Satan cannot stop your calling. Know that God's plans for you are good and He wants to use you to bless many lives.

"For I know the plans I have for you, says the Lord. They are plans for good and not for evil, to give you a future and a hope."

*– **Jeremiah 29:11**.*

Know that today is the day to answer God's call on your life.

Repeat this prayer: "Lord, remind me how brief my time on earth will be. Remind me that my days are numbered and that my life is fleeing away."

*– **Psalm 39:4***

Chapter 3

BECOMING AN EMPOWERED WOMAN

> *"The God who created, names and numbers the stars in the heavens also numbers the hairs on my head. He pays attention to very big things and to very small ones. What matters to me matters to Him, and that changes my life."*
>
> **– Elisabeth Elliot**

Women; the mothers, the daughters, the aunts, the wives, the grandmothers, the sisters, the entrepreneurs, the ministers, the planners, the ultimate nurturer.

The role of a woman is so dynamic and precious, and their contribution can never be measured. For years women have had to prove their worth and purpose; but we thank God, we are in an era where women are liberated and valued despite the odds.

The feminist movement has managed to gain some positive steps towards the equality of women, but as Christian women, we must be conscious of the fact that many of the current cultural norms of womanhood today are not biblical. As such, when we look at "empowerment" we do not accept the world's definition, but instead, we know and acknowledge our identity as found in Jesus Christ.

What is Empowerment?

Empowerment is the process of unleashing the power within us and using that power to make a positive impact. As women of God, true power only comes from the Holy

Spirit. It is His power that releases us to walk in true freedom, beauty and confidence.

It is only through His power that we can have transformational influence in our lives and in the lives of others.

Who is a Godly Empowered Woman?

A godly empowered woman is submitted to the Lordship of Jesus Christ. She knows she was made in His image (***Genesis 1:27***), and she has accepted the gift of salvation, where she has been redeemed (***Ephesians 1:7***).

Why are you Empowered for Such a Time as This?

When we look at our society today and how the women are now exhibiting themselves, it is heartbreaking that godly women are not boldly standing up for righteousness as we ought to.

Yes, many Christian women are doing well in their families, ministries and on the mission fields and we commend them, and we stay in prayer for the women who are walking in their God-given calling; but what about the others? The other Christian women that are comfortable with the cliché life; attending church weekly, doing devotionals, single women fixated on finding a husband; career women focused on getting a promotion, business women seeking after a six-figure salary, married women solely focused on her family. These are not bad things, but the question we should ask is, are we truly living the purposeful lives God has called us to live?

I believe that our young girls need to see godlier empowered women – women who are seeking the Kingdom first, loving and serving others, radiating true feminine beauty and confidently walking in their calling. Women they can use as an example.

The *Empowered* woman is who you see in the boardrooms, leading and representing amongst the men; she knows that the job doesn't define her, and she does it well. The *Empowered* woman is that woman you see in the political arena; the one leading a party, leading a community.

She is the woman you see in the courtroom as a Judge, an Attorney; you see her in the classroom, her head held high because she was determined to get that education that would secure her a place in the field of her dreams. The *Empowered* woman is a minister, a stay-at-home mom, a domestic helper, a secretary; she knows that her worth is not in her qualifications or her positions but that her identity is found in Christ.

Empowered women are God-centered, not self-centered. *Empowered* women are God-confident, not self-confident. *Empowered* women are God-motivated, not self-motivated. *Empowered* women trust the Lord with all their hearts and lean not on their own understanding.

Empowered women are standing up boldly for righteousness, holiness, and purity. *Empowered* women are led by the Holy Spirit, not by her emotions, culture or her fleshly desires, plans or dreams. *Empowered* women studies God's Word, live God's Word and preaches His undiluted Word.

Empowered women do not care about the world knowing her name as long as they know her God.

Yes!! I am praying that I will be that woman. What about you? Will you join me in this movement?

Here are Eight Practical Tips on Becoming an Empowered Woman

1. Put God First

> *"But seek first His kingdom and His righteousness, and all these things will be added to you."*
>
> *– Matthew 6:33*

The first step to becoming an *Empowered* woman is putting God first, above all else, and knowing that when you make your relationship with God your priority, everything else will fall into place.

There are so many things vying for our attention in the world today. It is so easy to get caught up in the distractions; our children, our jobs, our hobbies, our husbands, and even our ambitions. You must be intentional about putting God first and making Him a priority in your life. Make it your goal to have a deep, intimate relationship with Him. Let Him into every area of your life and decide to serve Him with your whole heart.

> *"Stop trying to fit [Christ] into your life; instead, build your life around [Him]."*
>
> **– Leslie Ludy**

Personal Reflection

Have you put God first in every area of your life? What areas could you release more control to God in?

2. Use Your Gifts to Serve

"As each has received a gift, use it to serve one another, as good stewards of God's varied grace."

– 1 Peter 4:10

An *Empowered* woman uses her God-given gifts to serve others wholeheartedly, and it brings glory to God. Your unique gift was given to you, not for yourself, but to build others and empower them.

There is no small gift; every gift is needed to play a part. There are no insignificant people in the family of God. Your gift is needed to make the world a better place. Spiritual gifts are not meant to draw attention to ourselves. God gives them to us, so we can bless and build others up.

You should glorify God in everything you do. This means not being limited to your prayers, attending church and reading the Holy Bible but also in your day to day service to others, through your gifts and talents.

Personal Reflection

How do you like to serve others? Is there a cause you feel passionate about?

_____
_____
_____
_____
_____
_____
_____
_____
_____
_____
_____
_____
_____
_____
_____
_____
_____
_____
_____

3. Believe you can accomplish your God-given Dreams.

*"I can do all things through Christ
who strengthens me"*

– Philippians 4:13

An *Empowered* woman knows that God placed her on this earth for a purpose. He has given you dreams and visions to accomplish the purpose, and although there will be challenges along the way; you should believe in yourself because you know that God has already equipped you.

Don't be afraid to go after your dreams. No dream is too big or unobtainable. An *Empowered* woman knows that she can accomplish anything she sets out to do. Write your vision and make it plain. Do not hold back! When you have a dream, and you know what you are working towards, this will motivate, empower and inspire you to effectively move forward with purpose.

> *"Everyone has inside of him a piece of good news. The good news is that you don't know how great you can be! How much you can love! What you can accomplish! And what your potential is!"*
>
> **Anne Frank**

Personal Reflection

What dream do you believe God has placed on your heart? What is stopping you from fulfilling it?

_____
_____
_____
_____
_____
_____
_____
_____
_____
_____
_____
_____
_____
_____
_____
_____
_____
_____
_____

4. Radiate Godly Beauty

> *"Charm is deceitful and beauty is vain, but a woman who fears the LORD, she shall be praised."*
>
> **– Proverbs 31:30**

An *Empowered* woman is not only admired for her physical appearance; she is admired for her inner qualities as well. She is tender-hearted, loving, nurturing and joyful.

Nothing is wrong with being physically attractive or adorning yourself fashionably yet modestly. Do not be enticed by the world's teaching of how women should dress or carry herself, or by the world's definition of beauty. Inward beauty comes from a relationship with God.

Personal Reflection

What is your definition of beauty? What are some of the characteristics you think a beautiful woman should radiate?

_____
_____
_____
_____
_____
_____
_____
_____
_____
_____
_____
_____
_____
_____
_____
_____
_____
_____
_____
_____

5. Complement Men, Not Compete

"The LORD God said, "It is not good for the man to be alone. I will make a helper suitable for him"

– Genesis 2:18

An *Empowered* woman knows that she is not in competition with her male counterpart; instead, she knows God placed her on this earth to complement him. She understands the value and strength that men possess and appreciates them and aspires to play the part she was created for.

You do not need to prove your worth as a woman to anyone. No, you are not a doormat, and no, you are not less than a man in anyway. Men and women have different roles to play in the society and the plan God has for your life is just right.

His plan is perfect.

Personal Reflection

Are there any godly examples of Christian marriages you know of? What do you admire about how these wives treat their husbands?

6. Empowers Other Women

"By this shall all men know that ye are my disciples, if ye have love one to another."

– John13:35

An *Empowered* woman encourages other women to strive for what they want. She doesn't pull people down but instead helps them to discover their full potential. Many women have a problem celebrating other women – her success, her happiness. It is easier for them to tear down, gossip about and glorify in the failures of another woman. Don't be that woman.

You *DO NOT* and *SHOULD NOT* have a reason to compare yourself to another woman. You know that God has a unique plan for your life. You should appreciate the accomplishments of others and celebrate their victories. Every victory of the empowered woman is a victory for God, and every victory for God, is a victory for His Kingdom.

Personal Reflection

Have you ever felt that you were in competition with another woman? Why do you think you felt that way? How can you deal with any feelings of jealousy or bitterness towards your sister?

_____

_____

_____

_____

_____

_____

_____

_____

_____

_____

_____

_____

_____

_____

_____

_____

_____

7. Recognize Your Calling

"For I know the plans I have for you," declares the LORD, "plans to prosper you and not to harm you, plans to give you hope and a future."

– Jeremiah 29:11

It is important for you to recognize and fulfill your God-given assignments. The calling on your life is significant, and there are people who are dependent on you playing your part. It is time to release self-doubts, negative people and their opinions and any insecurities that hold you back from sharing your gifts, talents, experiences, stories, testimonies, and passions with the world.

You were created for something, for a reason bigger than what you could fathom. *(Jeremiah 29:11).* You are not a mistake *(Jeremiah 1:5).* Don't let the devil turn you into to a spectator of life. Your life matters, and it must be lived to the fullest. God will never compare you to anybody else, but He is going to compare you to your potential.

No one can make the difference, only you can. You have unlimited potential within you. Assess your gifts and use them to build the Kingdom and serve others. Allow God to work through you. You are unique. You are called. You are special.

Be unapologetic about your calling. The world needs you. You don't need anyone's approval. **Jesus has already stamped APPROVED on your life.**

Personal Reflection

How can you stand in the power of your gift and calling and focus less on the negatives?

_____

_____

_____

_____

_____

_____

_____

_____

_____

_____

_____

_____

_____

_____

_____

8. Impact the World Positively

> *"You are salt for the earth. You are light for the world. A city cannot be hidden when it is located on a hill."*
>
> *– Matthew 5:13a, 14*

An *Empowered* woman is passionate about making a godly impact in this world. She knows her love for God inspires her to love others also, and this makes her want to share the Gospel with lost souls.

You are called to be a positive influence through giving back to others, caring for the poor and needy and opening your heart to helping others. It doesn't matter how small you think your act of kindness is, even a smile can make a big difference for someone.

Speak positively about others and share God's love and His message of salvation every chance you get.

Personal Reflection

Who do you think you are called to serve? For example, teenagers, elderly, single mothers, etc. What is one thing you can do to make a difference in someone's life this week?

Chapter 4

GOT IDOLS?

We have read so many stories of the Israelites and how they worshiped false idols even as God showed Himself so faithful to them over and over. Many scoff because we are not making a "golden calf" or bowing down before physical idols. But there are modern forms of idolatry now plaguing us and if we don't identify them, many of us will be caught in a form of godliness but denying God's power (**2 Tim 3:5**).

When I write, I always want to take the speck out of my eye first before I even consider addressing anyone about their actions.

At the end of August 2014, just before I went on a three (3) month social media fast, I kept finding excuses why I shouldn't do the fast, but God said I had to so, there was no excuse, and I could not change His mind. It was hard to fathom how I would manage not being on social media for three months, but I remember a friend said to me, "Crystal your phone is your idol." I thought "What?! How dare you say that?" He said anything that you spend more time with than God is an idol.

Honestly, I was offended. How could he say that to me? Who could love their phone more than God? But sadly he was right.

Modern-day idolatry doesn't come in the form of a statue or an image you bow down to. It is anything that can replace Jesus in your life.

I had many idols in my life, and honestly, I believe there are still some that as I grow in my relationship with God, He will reveal.

I want to share a few of mine with you, so you can know that you are not alone in this. I know how difficult it is to admit that a saved, sanctified woman of God like you can still have a heart of idolatry. But I've been there.

A few of my idols that God revealed to me over the years included:

a) Friendships – I had some of my friends on a pedestal to the point that even when I know God wanted me to stop partying, I couldn't because I was fearful that I would lose them if I did.

b) Education – Growing up I always felt that my only way out of poverty was through education, so I worked super hard to achieve all the necessary qualifications. This is not a bad thing normally, except when you are doing all of this to appear successful in the eyes of the world.

c) Relationships – I needed a boyfriend, seriously, I felt I just always needed to be in a relationship for whatever reason and of course none of these relationships were good for me because they all were contrary to God's Word.

d) Outer Appearance – Brazilian Hair, shortest outfits, whatever makes me feel good about myself when I look in the mirror. But even more fascinating to me was that the outfit got the most attention; what pictures got the most likes on social media. That was what I yearned for.

e) People-pleasing – Everything I did, my first response was what people would think about me. Yes, I would ponder about what Jesus' thoughts were, but people's thoughts and reactions were my first concern.

Honestly, my worth was tied up in ALL these things: what my friends thought of me. Why don't they want to be my friends anymore? Was I looking beautiful enough? Was I pleasing my boyfriend? Was I making 'my boo' happy? Do I look better than my boyfriend's ex-girlfriends? Was I spinning heads in the dance (sessions) or clubs? What other qualifications can I get to go higher in the company?

We have now created an idol of SELF! The world has become so materialistic that it builds our egos and forces us to want to acquire more material possessions. Some people must have the newest version cell phones, must own the biggest home; newer model cars, most expensive hair, clothes, and shoes.

These acquisitions are all because of covetousness and to gain admiration from the world. It is Satan's trap to keep our focus on ourselves and not on God, so we are busy with our careers, jobs, seeking higher accolades and relationships. All these things will have no eternal value because after we die, they're no use to us (***Ecclesiastes 2:21-23***).

I know so many women who want to give their lives to God but won't because they don't want to lose their boyfriends or baby fathers. I know so many young men and ladies who want to have a relationship with God but they are afraid to lose the friends they have, they don't want to stop partying or give up sex or drugs. Everybody wants to 'clean up' their lives first.

Girl, you have made this guy your god! You are doing everything you can to please him but he is still cheating; still disrespecting you and won't marry you because "he's not ready or he can't afford it yet." Sis, God loves you so much and He is so jealous over you.

I know how it feels to be afraid to let go. When I got saved I had to choose between an 8-year relationship (that was going nowhere) or God, who loves me even before I was in my mother's womb. I knew I needed a Savior. I knew the life I was living was leading me straight to hell!

You know you need Jesus to rescue you, to save you, to love you. What this man is offering is temporary my darling. Jesus is offering you eternity. I beg you to choose Him today!!

Believer, God is calling you to be Holy! That means you are called to be set apart from the world. God said, *"If any man loves the world, the love of the Father is not in Him"* (**1 John 2:15**). What He's saying here is that you cannot say you love Him and love the world at the same time.

It also means you should not be in that unequally yoked relationship; you cannot be in the club on Saturday night and stand on the church choir Sunday morning. It means you cannot be scantily clad because you are trying to fit in; it means you can't be so consumed about studying for your next exam that you don't even pray anymore.

People pleasing is idolatry. Peer pressure is idolatry. Your child, as simple as you take it, can become your idol. Your husband or wife can become your idol. Your career, car, family, cell phone or IPad can become your idol.

Our hearts and minds must be centered on God. Jesus said the greatest commandment is to,

"Love the Lord your God with all your heart and with all your soul and mind"

(Matthew 22;37).

When we love the Lord and try to obey His commands, there will be no room in our hearts for idolatry.

Let us pray:

Dear Abba Father, teach me to love You with all my heart, with all my soul and with all my mind. Help me to have a true heart of worship and diligently seek You every single day. Lord, I ask that You give me a new encounter with You and help me to have an authentic

relationship with You. God I ask You to increase my appetite for Your Word; let me hunger and thirst for Your righteousness and seek Your heart and not Your hands. Forgive me Jesus for being so caught up in temporary things. Holy Spirit lead me and have Your way. In Jesus' name. Amen

Chapter 5

COURAGE TO OBEY

When you think about an empowered woman, I am sure words like bold, courageous, fearless and confident are some of the words that may come to mind.

I'm sure you'll want to convince yourself that only certain women possess those characteristics but probably not you, right?

So I want you to pause right now and write the name of three empowered women you know (personally or not).

1. _____
2. _____
3. _____

Let me ask you this, did you write your own name? If you did, well congratulations to you! But I can tell you that 9 out of 10 women who do this exercise won't write their name. Why? We underestimate ourselves by comparing ourselves with others. We pay more attention to what others are doing and what others have accomplished but neglect to believe in ourselves and stay true to who we are.

I start here because this is our reality. We live in disobedience because many times we fear what others will think or say about us. We allow the perceived perceptions of others to dim our light and deter us from the greatness God has placed in us.

The difference between an empowered woman and a GODLY empowered woman is that the power and authority we possess as Christ-centered women does not come from "us"; this comes from the Holy Spirit, living in us!

Honestly, it's quite exhausting trying to do everything on my own. All the dreams I desire to achieve, really takes too much effort, time, strength and even money.

During this pursuit, I probably would have to sacrifice my family or relationships in order to "make it."

I believe in allowing the Holy Spirit living in me to lead me. He knows ALL things and He will and He can achieve far greater than I could in my own strength.

To allow the Holy Spirit to lead your life requires obedience. Not partial obedience (that's still disobedience) but total and complete obedience to God's will, laws, and plans.

It takes courage to be obedient to God

Obedience means to do what God says, how He says to do it and when He says to do it. It comes through surrender!

Obedience is not a destination; it's a life-long faith journey in your walk with Christ. With each step of obedience, you receive blessings and experience a freedom and peace that is unexplainable. Each and every day we should be praying and asking the Lord to show us what we are supposed to be doing!

Being obedient is not easy. We all have our selfish desires, and our own plans and obedience sometimes require us to do things we would rather not do. It comes from meditating on God's Word, listening to His voice, surrendering to His will and having a repentant heart.

Obedience requires trust, so if we don't know God, we can't trust Him. If we don't trust Him we won't surrender; if we don't surrender, then we can't obey.

(Jeremiah 1:9)

God has great plans for us. He has important things for us to do. He already has our destiny waiting on us, but it will require our obedience to get there.

When we obey, we gain clarity. So even if we don't see the big picture yet, because we know He is the GREATEST Father, He will never hurt us.

Being obedient comes with so many rewards including: answered prayers (***Psalm 66:18-19***), blessings (***Deuteronomy 11:26-27***), peace (***Psalm 37:37***) and safety (***Leviticus 25:18***).

In a conversation with Gary Messam from the God-Centered Ministry in Jamaica, he said as we walk in God's purpose, many times we don't know the impact of our obedience.

So as you are being empowered to walk in your calling, I want to encourage you to not think about yourself. Instead know that when you're obedient, it plays a major role in the advancement of God's kingdom on earth (no matter how small you believe the step is).

Personal Reflection

Is there any area in your life that you haven't totally surrendered to God?

_____

_____

_____

Can you think of a time you were obedient to God and things worked out better than you expected?

_____

_____

_____

What are the other rewards of being obedient?

_____

_____

_____

Chapter 6

POSITIONED FOR PURPOSE

There is constant talk about purpose. It has become the new "fad," where you hear so often that I want to search or pursue my purpose. In the Christian circle, when you hear about purpose, people refer to starting a ministry, writing a book, joining a praise team and all the "doing" stuff. Outside, the church arena, worldly people refer to purpose as "finding your center, passion or self-fulfillment."

Let's go to basics.

What is the meaning of "Purpose"?

The dictionary gives two forms and definitions of purpose.

1. Purpose (*n*) – reason for something existing. I call it the dormant purpose 'justification.' For example: Why do you have a car? Dormant Purpose – to transport/ to take you from one place to another

2. Purpose (*v*) – have as one's intention. I call this the active purpose 'objective.' For example: What do you do with a car? Active Purpose – you drive it.

Understanding these two examples, you get the picture that "purpose" is not just the DOING, but the doing now serves something deeper; it becomes the why behind you "doing" what you ought to do!

Let's look back at the modes of transportations as an example. Man realized there is a need to travel from one place to another (dormant purpose). So, for man to fulfill the purpose, he uses animals, bicycles, buses, trailers, cars, submarines, airplanes and helicopters (active purpose).

Each mode of transportation varies and are used in different conditions based on speed, accessibility, etc.

I've been asked the question, do I believe as humans (created beings), we have an ultimate purpose for life?

Now, I am not a purpose-guru, but I've sought God for years on this topic and done many biblical studies. My answer is based on my understanding and it's the best way I try to explain the complex topic of "purpose."

So, YES, I do believe we ALL have ONE 'dormant' purpose, which is to GLORIFY GOD. This means to fear Him, obey Him, worship Him and surrender to Him in all we do.

Ecclesiastes 12:13 states

"Let us hear the conclusion of the whole matter:
Fear God, and keep his commandments:
for this is the whole duty of man." KJV

But even though that's our true and ultimate purpose of being created; we are also created to DO something. This is to be active and contribute uniquely to the world.

This is where the confusion comes in; to understand our contribution (some people refer to it, as our CALLING).

What does it mean to be positioned?

To be positioned is to be placed where someone or something SHOULD be. It's the appropriate place.

When something is in position, we understand that it is in the right place at the right time. And when something is out of position, it has a negative impact on other people or things.

BEING IN POSITION IS KEY!

Here are some interesting facts about purpose:

1. It is not lost.
2. It is right there waiting for you to discover then pursue.
3. Too many Christians are dormant or out of position.
4. God didn't create spare people, so every single person has a purpose (active contribution to make).

Let me give you an example:

Christopher Columbus was said to have discovered Jamaica, but Jamaica wasn't lost. It has always been there, but he needed to get the right map, utilize his gifts, talents, and passions then step out in faith to discover what was already there.

He also had to seek the Queen's permission (who was his head at the time), and his ultimate goal for the trip was to "help" his head (the Queen/country) find another route way to trade. This is similar to our case.

OUR PURPOSE IS IN CHRIST

So, Christ had a purpose for us before we were born (*Jeremiah 1:5*). I know many gurus tell us to look into ourselves for purpose, which cannot be the case, because the manufacturer knows why He made the product; the product does not determine why it was made.

Even if we have an idea what contribution we should make, without Christ, our motives and desires are selfish and impure. We are sinful by nature and our thoughts are evil

(Romans 3:23 and Mark 10:18).

We must surrender our lives, dreams, plans and will to God. Through surrender Christ now lives in us and through the power of the Holy Spirit, He reveals who we are and what our true calling is. Remember, only God knows what He wants. So to glorify Him, we must fulfill His desires and not ours.

OUR PURPOSE IS BECOMING ALL GOD HAS CALLED US TO BE

Here's the thing. We should not seek purpose, we should SEEK GOD and He will reveal the purpose to us.

Some facts about purpose:

1. Many times, we are busy seeking purpose, and not the purpose-giver Himself.

2. Many of us seek purpose for fame, stage or ministry. We must accept that some of us are bicycles, bikes, trailers, airplanes or submarines. Our contribution will look different and be different even though it's one main purpose.

3. Purpose is not just about "doing" but the WHY behind what we do is important. We must learn to glorify God where we are and with what we have.

4. Purpose is becoming all you were born to be. This is a life-long process, but God will use our unique experiences, gifts, talents, and passions to radiate who He is.

How do you discover purpose?

- You must ACCEPT Jesus Christ as Lord and Savior (be born-again) – ***John 3:3, 1 Peter 1:2-4***

- Let go of all you think you want to do or who you think you are. Fully surrender your all to Jesus and allow Him to lead you.

- Pray until it is revealed to you, but ensure you're being obedient in every single stage as He leads.

- Remember, it's not a comparison or competition game.

- Delight yourself in Christ – place every day, every need, every situation, dream or plan in His hands. Receive His love, peace, joy, and purpose.

PURPOSE IS NOT ABOUT YOU

Purpose has nothing to do with us; God uses us to show who He is to others. Our purpose is to glorify God – we can do this through our worship, giving, serving, singing, evangelizing, writing, dancing, cooking, and fellowship.

WHERE YOU ARE NOW, YOU ARE POSITIONED

Understand that positioning is not so much where you are physically; it is where you are mentally and spiritually.

As children of God, we must have faith that where we are physically, God allowed it for a specific reason. He wants us to learn where we are, which will prepare us for the next season in our life.

So even if you run away like Jonah and get caught in the belly of a big fish, remember God "positioned" him there to bring him to repentance so he could eventually go deliver the message to the people of Nineveh.

Even if people who intended to cause you harm, like Joseph's brother who threw him in a pit, God "positioned" him so he would eventually get to the palace where he was able to save his family.

Even if you're like Paul, busy doing the work of the Lord and being faithful to God, and you get thrown into prison, remember God "positioned" him there because in the prison, he was able to write the letters to the churches, which is a majority of the New Testament being read today.

WHAT A MIGHTY AND FAITHFUL GOD WE SERVE

Where you are positioned, you have a choice to live daily and make a decision to invest in building God's kingdom.

I want you to pause now and go read the book of Esther.

As I conclude this chapter, let me share some takeaways from the story of Esther in the Bible:

1. God is always in control and working behind the scenes. God has placed us where we are because He has 'purposed' us to be there (***Proverbs 19:21***). So your job, family, church, community or ministry is orchestrated by God.

2. God doesn't care about your past. He uses ALL of us uniquely. Esther was an orphan. Whatever you've been through God allowed it because He can and He will use it only for His true and divine purposes (***Romans 8:28***).

3. God looks at the internal; people look at the eternal. Your gifts and talents will open doors

but only your character will sustain you. Why are you doing what you are doing? The why (motive) behind what you are doing is more important than what you are doing. (*1 Samuel 16:7*) Esther's beauty got her in the Kingdom, but her love for people was what God used to save a nation.

4. Fasting and Prayer are essential to our walk. Esther sought God for direction before she made a move. Every move we make, we must seek God to lead the way.

5. NOW, is the time to pursue purpose. Too many times people remain stagnant or step out of position. We know we have a contribution to make, but we are waiting on something "deep" before we do anything.

BE CAREFUL THAT YOUR DREAM DON'T BECOME AN IDOL

Don't confuse your dream with your purpose; because it's easy for us to divert. If it doesn't glorify God, then it's not your purpose.

Yes, your dream can be your purpose, but surrender the dreams and ask God to take away the ones that are not from Him. Even when we are pursuing our purpose, continue surrendering to God. He wants us to cling to Him and not to our purpose or our dreams. They can easily turn into idols.

So where can you begin?

1. Intercede for others.
2. Spend time discovering your passions, gifts, and talents.
3. Reflect on past experiences you have learned from that you can share with others.
4. Serve wholeheartedly.
5. Remember, it's not about being busy, but it's about being productive in what you ought to be doing.
6. Evangelize and share the Gospel of Jesus Christ.

After reading this chapter, I pray it will challenge you to evaluate your current situation and help you recognize how important your contribution on earth is. God has a purpose for you and where you are now is preparing you for where He wants to take you. What you have been through will not be wasted, and somebody can be blessed by your lessons if you are willing to be obedient.

(In a later chapter, we'll talk more about using your mess and making it your message).

Personal Reflection

Are you having difficulty accepting your station in life? Do you resent where God has placed you?

_____

_____

What are some of the things you are thankful for in this season?

Where in your daily routine can you give God more glory?

How can you focus more on God even if things aren't going how you want them?

_____

_____

_____

_____

_____

Do you believe where you are currently positioned is where God wants you to be? Why or why not?

_____

_____

_____

_____

_____

Do you know your purpose in life? If not, where can you start? If yes, how have you been walking in that purpose?

_____

_____

_____

_____

_____

Chapter 7

DEFINING SUCCESS GOD'S WAY

Success is rarely discussed in the Christian circle because it is considered a 'worldly' thing. When we hear success; riches, luxury cars, popularity and awards come to mind. As Christians, we know these things don't matter as much as our relationship with God and being obedient to His will.

"So we make it our goal to please him."

(2 Corinthians 5:9a NIV)

As a godly empowered woman, I believe it is crucial that we understand what Christ-centered success looks like. In the above verse, we learn that our main goal should be to PLEASE GOD.

In our culture, we're constantly being told that we should "have it our way," "pursue our goals and dreams," "be better than others" and it becomes ALL about us. We then try to include God in our plans, especially when it seems like it's not working out for us. This should not be.

I tried not to share too much of my opinion, especially in this chapter, because for topic I spent weeks studying what other godly men and women has shared. More importantly, I spent time studying God's Word and seeking the Holy Spirit on His wisdom.

What is true success?

> *"Be strong and very courageous. Be careful to obey all the instructions Moses gave you. Do not deviate from them, turning either to the right or to the left. Then you will be successful in everything you do. Study this Book of Instruction continually. Meditate on it day and night so you will be sure to obey everything written in it. Only then will you prosper and succeed in all you do."*
>
> *– Joshua 1:7-8*

Prosperity and success do not come from power, influence, contacts or relentless desires to get ahead. It comes from obeying God's word! You must examine whose approval is more important to you. Is it God's or people?

God measures success by obedience, faithfulness, and righteousness. If you're faithfully doing the work God has given you to do, then you are a success in God's eyes.

Don't allow popularity to twist the perception of your importance. It is easy to be humble when you're not the center of attention, but the real test comes when you're being praised and recognized. Will you remain humble?

In his book, **_Success God's Way_**, Charles Stanley says:

> *"Our human approach to success tends to be: here's my goal. God's approach is: here's the person I want you to be, here's what I want you to do, and here's how to be that type of person and how to do that task. It is in being a godly person and then obeying God in His directives that we find success as Christians. Our life as Christians is not to be wrapped up in what we possess, earn or own. Life for Christians is wrapped up in who we are in Christ Jesus."*

SUCCESS BEGINS WITH RECEIVING GOD'S GIFT OF SALVATION

Understand that success comes from pleasing God. It is a journey of becoming who God has called you to be and accomplishing the goals God has given you to pursue. An ungodly person cannot be "successful." It is more than accomplishing wealth, fame, awards, status or power. It is more than setting a goal and accomplishing it. They are achieving their goals, and not God's goals for their life.

Similarly, for the persons who call themselves Christians – if you're leaving God out of your plans and not accomplishing His purpose, then you are not successful from God's viewpoint.

Being consistent leads to success.

> *"God is for your success in life; He created you for a purpose and he wants you to succeed. It is God, your Creator, who will measure your success in life, and no one else."*
>
> **– Rick Warren**

Success is not a destination. You can be successful at any stage of your life, based on your values and goals.

Having discipline is important to success.

> *"Being successful and fulfilling your life's purpose is not at all the same thing; you can reach all your personal goals, become a raving success by the world's standards, and still miss your purpose in this life."*
>
> **– Rick Warren**

In the drive for success, keep your ambition under God's control. It is okay for Christians to desire ambition, and for us to be industrious, but obedience and service come first. (***Matthew 9:34, Matthew 6:33***)

Always acknowledge God as the center of your success. (***1 Chronicles 18:13***). Always remember that true success is a blessing from the Heavens.

SEEK EXCELLENCE, NOT SUCCESS

Instead of seeking success, seek excellence. Out of excellence comes success!

Is it your desire to become a woman of excellence?

_____

_____

_____

_____

_____

_____

According to Bishop Omar Wedderburn – the chase of success many times becomes discouraging because it becomes a race of attainment, power and fame. Instead of striving for success, strive for excellence.

This is challenging you to not attain "things" but to build character. On the journey of becoming a woman of excellence, you become the best that God has called you to be.

Instead of comparing yourself to others, you're tapping into the unlimited potential God has available for you.

Vivian Jokotade's 3 Recipe for Success

1. HAVE A VISION – You will succeed as you see. See yourself as a visionary woman. See

yourself as a successful woman. See yourself as a purposeful woman.

2. BE HUNGRY – Get hungry for your success. This is not success defined by others (it's becoming the woman God has called you to be.) Success is God-given, but it is up to you to make it happen.

3. PLAN – You will succeed as much as you schedule. Get organized and manage your time wisely.

7 Characteristics of A Godly Successful Woman

1. Righteousness (Proverbs 12:3)
2. Honesty (Proverbs 13:5)
3. Commit all her work to God (Proverbs 16:3)
4. Seek God's Wisdom (Proverbs 19:8)
5. Humility (Proverbs 22:4)
6. Fear of God (Proverbs 31:30)
7. Confess her sins (Proverbs 28:13)

Personal Reflection

How do you define SUCCESS?

_____

_____

_____

_____

What does success in your life look like?

___

___

___

___

___

___

What are some differences between setting "worldly" and "godly goals"?

___

___

___

___

___

___

Where in your life do you struggle most with discipline? Why?

_____

_____

_____

_____

_____

_____

What are some ways you can grow in your discipline?

_____

_____

_____

_____

_____

_____

Chapter 8

TURNING YOUR MESS INTO A MESSAGE

Can you see that our messes are not unique to us? There is someone else, somewhere else, that has faced something similar who still feels trap. What if you could provide hope for them? Will you be willing to?

This chapter could be retitled, *"Turn your pain into purpose," "Turn your test into a testimony," "Turn your fears into faith," "Turn your struggle into success,"* or *"Turn a victim into a victory!"*

However, you want to say it, **GOD CAN WORK IT ALL OUT AND MAKE IT BRAND NEW!**

"And we know that in all things God works for the good of those who love Him, who have been called according to His purpose"

– Romans 8:28

Before we get into the depth of this chapter, let us first agree on these truths:

- God has a plan for your life.
- You have many gifts and talents.
- You are not an accident.
- You are called to live a life of purpose.
- You have a contribution to make.
- What God will do with you is unique.

Chapter 8: Turning Your Mess into A Message

- This world is not your home.
- Your life should bring glory to God.
- Jesus is more than enough.
- You cannot know your purpose, if you don't know God.
- You don't know God unless you accept His gift of salvation through Jesus Christ.
- Life is all about love.
- God is LOVE.
- You need others in your life.
- You were created to become like Christ.
- There is purpose behind every problem.
- You are a solution to a problem.
- Someone is depending on your obedience.
- Faith pleases God.

I could go on, but you get the picture.

> *"Through salvation our past has been forgiven, our present is given meaning and our future is secured."*
>
> **– Rick Warren**

In this life, we will experience many pains and troubles; people will hurt us, and we will hurt people. We will fail many of life's tests, but we will also pass many too. There will be struggles that we will go through, but it is not constant, we will get through it.

We will make bad decisions and get ourselves into messes, but if we allow God to work in us and through us, there will be something beautiful at the end.

I can confidently tell you that God is in the restoration business. Nothing is wasted with Him. It doesn't matter who you are, what you've done, or what has been done to you, God is willing and able to make all things new.

"Behold, I will do a new thing; now it shall spring forth; shall ye not know it? I will even make a way in the wilderness, and rivers in the desert"

– Isaiah 43:19

Don't allow your mistakes to rule you. Don't allow your past to control your future. No, it may not be good what you did and yes, you probably should have handled it better, but it doesn't stop God's plan for your life.

Staying in your mess will remind you of who you once were and who you used to be. Your message is the insight, wisdom or experience that someone else needs.

The purpose of our mistake is to learn from it and allow God to make something beautiful from our brokenness.

Would you believe me if I told you it is the lesson learned from our mess that creates the platform for us to walk into our destiny?

I wonder what freedom would look like if we chose to surrender and see that God can handle it and still work it out for our good?

How to turn your mess into a message

1. Admit that something was done wrong to you or you did something wrong.

2. Pray and release your sins to God.

3. Evaluate the lessons you've learned or the victory you've won.

4. Spend time with Jesus and falling in love with Him.

5. Ask God for the courage to share your story with someone.

True freedom requires the courage to embrace what happened to you and use it to change the world. There is no greater comfort to someone who is suffering, than another person who has been through similar or the same situation and survived, and is willing to take their hand and guide them out of the dark.

6. Ask yourself if you've become passionate about anything from that experience.

7. Think about the bigger vision. No matter what's happened in your life, your story isn't finished

yet. We all need time to heal from the messes of our lives, but after we've healed, we need to consider re-investing our hearts with a bigger plan and purpose in mind.

8. Don't ever give up. He is waiting on you to step out in faith and trust Him to lead you. He is waiting for your first move. He will meet you when you move.

It's okay to mess up as long as you get back up. Actually people are more likely to listen and learn from your personal failures rather than from your success. We are all connected in some of the same ways. You never know who may need to hear your testimony because they are experiencing something similar. So when God allows you to make it through something tough, don't shy away - share it! You never know who your story may help!"

– Rachel Proctor

Dear Heavenly Father,

For so many years I've lived under the shame, regret, and burdens from my past mistakes. I thank You for Your forgiveness. I thank You for Your healing. Today I offer myself up to You. I trust You can and You will turn my mess into my message. In Jesus' name, Amen.

Personal Reflection

What are some of the mistakes you've made in life and what have you learned from them?

_____

_____

_____

_____

_____

_____

What are some of the tests life has forced you to take and what lessons have you learned?

_____

_____

_____

_____

_____

_____

What are some of the pains you've experienced *(things done by others that hurt you)* and how did you overcome? If you haven't overcome yet what is the first step you can make towards your healing?

_____

_____

_____

_____

_____

_____

What are you most passionate about?

_____

_____

_____

_____

_____

_____

Who are you most passionate about helping?

_____

_____

_____

_____

_____

_____

Based on all the lessons you have learned in life so far, which one stands out the most to you?

_____

_____

_____

_____

_____

_____

What do you believe is your message to the world?

_____

_____

_____

_____

_____

_____

(In different seasons our messages might change but don't try to convince yourself that you don't have a message, because we have all gone through something).

Name three people you believe you can share your message (testimony) with.

_____

_____

_____

_____

_____

_____

Crafting Your Purpose Statement

Fill in the blanks for 1, 2, 4 and 5. Circle ONE of the terms in 3 that best describes what you would love to see yourself doing. Once you have worked through the template, place your responses in the spaces provided below.

Don't take it too seriously. It's not set in stone, so get creative with this and be very prayerful about it.

(1) My name is _____

(2) and I help (Whoever is your target audience) _____

_____

Who

(3) (love/hate/need/can't figure out how

to/struggle with/are looking for/ready for)

(4) Problem they have

_____

(5) So that (result)

_____

Example: *My name is Crystal Daye and I help women who struggle with purpose, identity and confidence so that they can live wholesome godly lives*

In my personal purpose statement:

- Target audience: **women**
- What is their issue: **struggle with**
- Problem: **their purpose, identity, and confidence**
- Result they receive: **to live wholesome godly lives.**

Complete Yours:

_____
_____
_____
_____
_____
_____
_____
_____
_____

Examples of persons I admire that have impacted me with their message and have birth ministries from it:

- *Heather Lindsey* shares her struggles with fornication and how God led her to living a pure life and the birth of *Pinky Promise Ministry*.

- *Joyce Myers* shares her story of being abused by her dad, and now she writes books and ministers to people all over the world.

- *Sarah Jakes* got pregnant as a teenager, being the daughter of a prominent Pastor, and even experienced a failed marriage and now she ministers to others.

- *Crisha Bowen* from Trinidad shares her story of having achieved the success she thought she wanted (education and a great job) yet she felt empty until she found purpose in Christ and now she helps others find their purpose.

- *Carla Dunbar*, a Jamaican Pastor and Marriage counselor shares her story of living with her boyfriend from her teenage years. Even as a Pastor her husband was unsaved and committed adultery. She chose to forgive him and now she helps other marriages to heal from infidelity.

- *Raquel Jones*, ordained Apostle and famously known for reading the news on a popular Jamaican television station, shares how she lost two of her fingers, on her left hand, in a shooting accident as a teenager and felt inadequate for many years. Now she ministers the Gospel of Christ all over the world.

I also want to share a few women who didn't have a major platform but in their own way of trying to live a life of purpose and obedience, have made an impact.

Annette Williams, my best friend Tashna's mom, is a simple dressmaker who desired to dedicate her life to ensuring her daughter who lived in the inner city didn't turn out a statistic. I don't know much about Ms. Annette, but what I admired was how she believed, even as a single mother, that her main priority was to ensure that her daughter had a relationship with God.

Two women from my former church, **Sister Lola and Sister Nikki**, through their life of walking with God showed me what the power of a praying woman looks like. They were not just dedicated to praying for themselves and their families, but continuously interceded for their church family, the country and just about everyone they came across.

Finally, my aunt, **Bobbet.** She is one of the most dedicated Christian women I know growing up. She faithfully wakes up at 5am every day to read her Bible and pray. Her life was dedicated to serving at church and living a godly life.

There are many other examples of godly empowered women I could share with you; but I am sure you also know other women that have impacted you with their story and life of obedience to God.

Let me share a little about my journey with you:

After I re-dedicated my life to the Lord on January 1, 2014, I was constantly pursuing God to reveal my purpose. At a Women's Retreat, I shared with the ladies my passion for helping young ladies become confident and fulfill their dreams. This birthed the She's Royal Ministry.

Through this ministry, I've staged conferences, workshops and other events that impact many lives locally and internationally.

On November 30, 2014, after completing a 3-month social media fast, I preached my first sermon, which was the beginning of my speaking ministry.

In January 2015, I launched my blog which resulted in me writing books and devotionals. Since the release of my 1st book, "Living A Royal Reality" in August 2016, my company DayeLight International was found.

Honestly, these weren't my plans – these were all HIS plans. I could not have orchestrated all these blessings if I wanted to. It came from surrendering my ways for His. I had to be willing to allow Him to turn my mess into a powerful message that continues to impact women all over the world, even today.

Now I don't believe everyone will start a ministry or write a book or blog or start a business, but remember where you are positioned is where God wants to use you. So whether you're in an organization as a career woman, in the marketplace as a kingdom entrepreneur, school as a teacher or student, church as a minister or the cleaning lady, hospital as the medical professional, chef in a hotel, secretary for a government organization, mother at home with 3 children, you have a contribution to make, and you have been called FOR SUCH A TIME AS THIS!

Chapter 9

TRUTH ABOUT SELF-LOVE

First, I looked up the definition of self-love. Dictionary.com says, *"Self-love is a belief you hold that you are worthy and valuable."*

Now, is there anywhere in the Bible that says we are worthy or valuable? I would say look to the Cross! Jesus died because He saw us worthy and valuable to Him.

Here's the thing, as believers we know the "world" perverts everything. There is a worldly view of success, which is success defined by money and accolades. There is a worldly view of sex, which is, if I'm ready to have sex, just do it. There is a worldly view of purpose, which is defined by finding passion and happiness.

All these views are not biblical. It is the world's way, which is a lie and we know who is the father of lies right?

Well, we can view "Self-love" the same way. The world will have their own definition, which is self-focus and selfishness. They see self-love as a way to see themselves even above others and the Bible warns us against this (***1 Corinthians 13:4-6, Romans 2:8***).

"Do nothing from selfish ambition or conceit, but in humility count others more significant than yourselves."

– *Philippians 2:3*

But, I do believe there is a balanced biblical view for loving oneself. Here's the thing, sometimes in church we are taught what not to do and all the don'ts of life; but many church leaders fail to teach us the do's of life.

So while we are saying NO to the world's view of self-love, we should teach that we should see ourselves as God sees us (Take some time to reflect on *Psalm 139*).

- God has a plan for our lives (*Jeremiah 29:11*).
- God wants to have a relationship with us (*John 17:3*).
- His beautiful Spirit lives in us (*John 14:16-17*).
- We are made in the image and likeness of God (*Genesis 1:27*).

These scriptures tell us that we do matter to God. And if the Creator of the Universe sees us as valuable, worthy and beautiful, isn't it a sin for us to view ourselves any less?

We should look to the Cross for our identity and acceptance. When you do this, you have no premise to see others less than you are or to focus on yourselves. This view of "self-love" or loving yourself should propel you to truly love others as Christ loves us (*Mark 12:30-31*); because we know He has made us all uniquely and wonderfully.

One of the beautiful things about how Jesus taught while He was on the earth was that He shared "how" we should DO things and not just focus on the "what" alone as the law did, by pointing out all the don'ts.

So, how do we truly love ourself?

Through seeing yourself through God's eyes. As you the read the scriptures, God has shared so many promises and compliments about how He sees us. Read them. Reflect on them. Believe them.

So, yes I've seen the many arguments of believers saying all the reasons promoting "self-love" is wrong; and I understand that the constant message can be ungodly in some aspects. But there are many women sitting in church for years and never tap into their God-given potential and promises because they still feel rejected, unloved, ugly and useless.

Many of us don't know who we are in Christ and accept that He has a custom-made purpose specially made for us, so we constantly yearn to be like others and struggle with jealousy and covetousness.

Therefore, we should spend time in God's word so our minds can be renewed daily

(Romans 12:2).

Let's start to see ourselves as God sees us and realize that we must respect and love others because they are also uniquely loved and made in the image of God.

I don't believe loving ourselves is a sin. But if we make it become our focus and start to see ourselves as mini-gods or become self-absorbed, then that's where sin comes in.

Chapter 9: Truth About Self-love

But here's my thought on true "self-love" – **it's not about loving who we "are" instead loving who God created us to be.**

Recently, I said to a friend that Crystal without Christ is HORRIBLE. Yes, I mean without Jesus, my thoughts, actions and words were selfish, worldly-driven, lustful and downright dirty (***Isaiah 64:6***), but I THANK GOD FOR SALVATION!

Having a relationship with Christ has really been the best thing to happen to me, because I was truly horrible. Now, I am not saying I am sinless now, but the BLOOD has really cleansed me, so daily I am learning to rely on His Spirit to lead and renew me *(sanctification)*.

So, now I don't love old "Crystal" as she was, but I love the Crystal I am becoming (that God has created me to be). The one who has been blood-washed, re-born, made righteous, made worthy and is quite valuable in Jesus Christ.

That means, I try not to make excuses about my "dirty" ways and say that's just me! I know any character or habits that are unpleasing to God and that does not align with His character, is not who I am supposed to be.

So, lying, anger, bitterness, jealousy, selfishness, pride, being unkind, unforgiving, arrogant and lustful; the person we are naturally should not be accepted and lovable to us. These are the sinful images adopted from Adam through sin. This is why we needed a Savior.

What's the truth about self-love? You can only love yourself authentically through the LOVE OF GOD. That means we are trusting and relying on His LOVE to help us see ourselves differently. You cannot rely on yourself. You cannot rely on your strengths or qualifications to help you to "love yourself." We rely on Jesus Christ: in Him lies our identity, worth, and purpose.

It comes down to not loving "me" *per se*, but loving God and accepting Christ's sacrifice on the Cross. It's all about Him anyway!!

"But he that glorieth, let him glory in the Lord."

– *2 Corinthians 10:7*

Chapter 10

EMPOWERED WOMAN RESOURCE GUIDE

This guide includes:

a) Daily Habits of An Empowered Woman.

b) Inspirational Quotes.

c) Self- Reflection Journal Questions.

d) 10 Scriptures for An Empowered Woman.

e) 31-Day Biblical Affirmation

Daily habits of an empowered woman

- *Keep a close relationship with God.*
- *Talk to God about everything.*
- *Read God's Word daily.*
- *Be Thankful Always.*
- *Smile Often.*
- *Wear attire that reflects godliness and virtue.*
- *Take care of your body.*
- *Be a good steward of your finances.*
- *Get adequate rest.*
- *Make journaling a habit.*
- *Pray without ceasing.*
- *Pray for others.*
- *Serve others with your gifts and talents.*

- *Stop speaking negatively.*
- *Refrain from gossiping.*
- *Find a godly mentor.*
- *Be a godly mentor (find a mentee).*
- *Set measurable goals.*
- *Pursue your God-given dreams.*
- *Be kind to others.*
- *Stop Worrying.*
- *Live Purposefully.*
- *Love Others unconditional.*
- *Allow the Holy Spirit to lead you.*
- *Walk in Purity.*
- *Be a good friend.*
- *Surround Yourself with persons passionate about God.*
- *Stop Comparing Yourself to others.*
- *Guard your heart.*
- *Create healthy boundaries.*
- *Work as unto the Lord.*
- *Join a Bible-teaching church.*
- *Honor your parents.*

- ***Respect your leaders.***
- ***Invest in yourself.***
- ***Have fun!***

Inspirational Quotes for the Empowered Woman

"We will never be happy until we make God the source of our fulfillment and the answer to our longings. He is the only one who should have power over our souls."

– Stormie Omartian

"A godly woman is beyond average because she keeps her word. She honors her vows. She exhibits great faith. She overcomes great obstacles. And she affects her family, her community, even the world."

– Elizabeth George

"Salvation is a lifestyle of waking up and choosing God every single day of your life. As you CHOOSE to live for Him, He leads and guides your life."

– Heather Lindsey

"The fact that I am a woman does not make me a different kind of Christian, But the fact that I am a Christian does make me a different kind of woman."

– ***Elisabeth Elliot***

"You will begin to heal when you let go of the things that hurt you in the past, forgive those who have done wrong to you and learn to forgive yourself for the mistakes you have made."

– ***Crystal Daye***

"I have to keep reminding myself: If you give your life to God, He doesn't promise you happiness and that everything will go well. But He does promise you peace. You can have peace and joy, even in bad circumstances."

– ***Patricia Heaton***

"Being a praying woman doesn't mean I don't have bad days. It means I am willing to find beauty, even in the ugliest days."

– ***Unknown***

"Do what you can! If you can't feed 100 people, then feed just one."

– ***Mother Teresa***

> *"Being busy without a clear PURPOSE is like doing the backstroke in a community pool. Lots of movement, activity, and exertion of energy but NO FORWARD MOVEMENT! Get clear on where you're headed. Seek GOD for purpose in what you do. Don't let it be done in vain!"*
>
> *– **Rachel Proctor***

Self-Reflection Journal Questions for The Empowered Woman

How can you serve others with your gifts and talents right now?

_____

_____

_____

_____

_____

_____

Have you accepted Jesus as your Lord and Savior? If yes, do your day-to-day life reflect this? If not, what is stopping you?

_____

_____

_____

What fears, and roadblocks are in the way of living your purpose?

When you envision yourself as an Empowered woman, what does she look like?

How would you define personal success? Are your ideals more materialistic or intrinsic?

_____

_____

_____

_____

_____

_____

Write about something you need to be doing more often.

_____

_____

_____

_____

_____

_____

List five positive things about yourself and five areas you could work on.

_____

_____

_____

_____

_____

Name three ways you could be more selfless.

_____

_____

_____

_____

_____

_____

List five things you take for granted that others would be grateful for.

_____

_____

_____

_____

_____

_____

When you look in the mirror, describe the woman you see.

_____

_____

_____

_____

_____

Write about a bad decision you made in the past and what you learned from it.

_____
_____
_____
_____
_____
_____
_____

What does it mean to be a follower of Christ? Make five points.

_____
_____
_____
_____
_____
_____

10 Scriptures for Empowered Woman

Proverbs 31:30: Charm is deceitful and beauty is vain, but a woman who fears the LORD, she shall be praised.

Proverbs 31:26: She speaks with wisdom and faithful instruction is on her tongue.

Titus 2:3-5: Older women likewise are to be reverent in their behavior, not malicious gossips nor enslaved to much wine, teaching what is good, so that they may encourage the young women to love their husbands, to love their children, to be sensible, pure, workers at home, kind, being subject to their own husbands, so that the word of God will not be dishonored.

Galatians 5:16: So I say, walk by the Spirit, and you will not gratify the desires of the flesh.

Colossians 3:18: Wives, submit yourselves to your husbands, as is fitting in the Lord.

Proverbs 3:5: Trust in the LORD with all your heart and lean not on your own understanding.

Philippians 4:8: Finally, brothers and sisters, whatever is true, whatever is noble, whatever is right, whatever is pure, whatever is lovely, whatever is admirable—if anything is excellent or praiseworthy—think about such things.

Proverbs 1:7: The fear of the LORD is the beginning of knowledge, but fools despise wisdom and instruction.

1 Timothy 3:11: Women must likewise be dignified, not malicious gossips, but temperate, faithful in all things.

1 Timothy 2:9-10: Likewise, I want women to adorn themselves with proper clothing, modestly and discreetly, not with braided hair and gold or pearls or costly garments, but rather by means of good works, as is proper for women making a claim to godliness.

31- Day Biblical Declarations for An Empowered Woman

God loves me.
(1 John 4:16)

I love God.
(1 John 5:3; 2 John 1:6)

God has a good and perfect plan for my life.
(Jer. 29:11)

I love me.
(Mark 12:31)

I am beautiful.
(Gen. 1:27; Ps. 139:14; Eccl. 3:11)

*God has blessed me with all I need
to fulfill His will for my life.*
(2 Peter 1:3)

*God finishes what He starts and
He began a good work in my life.*
(Phil. 1:6)

*I'm a godly (holy, pure, righteous),
God-fearing woman.*
(Prov. 31:10; 1 John 5:3)

*God loves me and I have His approval,
and that is all that truly matters.*
(2 Tim. 2:15)

*God is faithful and always keeps His word.
Even unto me!*
(Ps. 89:8; Matt. 7:21)

*In Jesus I have the victory;
therefore, I cannot lose.*
(1 Cor. 15:57)

I am a winner with Jesus.
(1 Cor. 15:57)

God is in control. His will,
which is also my will, will be done.
(1 John 5:14-15)

When I obey God it means that I trust Him.
(Zeph. 3:2)

Jesus will never leave me.
(Matt. 28:20)

I will not fear. I am not afraid.
I choose to no longer be bound by fear.
(2 Tim. 1:7)

God will turn all bad in my life into good for me.
(Rom. 8:28)

Everything happens for a reason or
for my learning.
(Eccl. 3:17)

God is listening to and answering my prayers.
(Ps. 4:3)

There is nothing God can't do.
(Matt. 19:26)

No weapon formed against me shall prosper.
(Isa. 54:17)

Everything God has belongs to me.
(Gal. 4:7)

Today I will be grateful, hopeful,
and faithful and therefore joyful!
(Ps. 132:16; Eccl. 2:26)

God's way is best and always will be.
(1 Cor. 1:25)

The highest honor is being a godly woman.
(Prov. 31:10, 30-31)

Father God created me to do good works.
(Eph. 2:10)

I am beloved and precious to God.
(Ps. 72:14; 1 Peter 2:4)

God will fight all my battles—all I need to do is obey and get out of the way.
(1 Peter 5:7)

Because of Jesus, I have free access to God.
(1 Tim. 2:5; 1 Peter 2:5)

If I do not feel happy or joyful, it's most likely because I am not walking in the Spirit, which is love, joy, peace, patience, kindness, goodness, faithfulness, gentleness, and self-control.

(Gal. 5:22-23)

LETTER TO ROYALTIES: A SURRENDERED LIFE

Jesus wants us to be more than saved. He wants us to be surrendered to Him. It's not easy to make a full surrender; sometimes it's even painful.

As humans, we naturally have our own desires, dreams, and plans. Nothing is wrong with that, as long as it fits into God's will, which is the best plan for our lives.

> *Even though God doesn't owe you anything,*
> *He has given you everything.*

God has given you gifts so you can live a life of purpose, impact, and potential. It's often uncomfortable to trust God and follow His plan if you're not growing in intimacy with Him and accept that He's Sovereign and He knows best.

Don't let fear control you and hinder you from living a life filled with God's unlimited favor and blessings.

As a woman of faith driven by purpose and obedience, you are challenged to forsake worldly pursuits and build your life as His priority. Yes, your main aim is to cultivate an intimate relationship with Christ, but it means becoming His light to this dying world.

You are commissioned to share the Gospel while using your gifts and story to impact the world for the glory of God.

> *"God will make up in ability at
> the level of your availability."*
>
> **– Chris Benton**

Ladies, this is our time!!

Discover how you can make a difference. Embrace your calling as women to impact the world for the glory of God.

Every day we live, and every decision we make is an investment. Everything you do is an investment: the movies you watch, the friends you hang with and everything you pursue. We are either investing in a temporary stock of today's pleasure or eternal stock of looking forward to greater.

FOR SUCH A TIME AS THIS is investing in today

Learning to live well today, because today was given to us to bring glory to God. Regardless of what you have been through, today is the day you can change the view.

You are empowered to live a royal life, fulfill your unique calling and finding your destiny in the Kingdom of God.

CONCLUSION

I believe that the word "empowered" is not a bad word; but if we allow the world to define it, it will be contrary to what the Bible teaches and as women of God, the Word of God is the standard we ought to live by.

A Christian empowered woman's values, identity, purpose, and worth comes from the Word. She is expected to portray femininity despite her position or status. How she dresses, behaves or speaks must represent godliness and virtue.

She is spiritually strong and her life is centered around God, His commands, and plans. Even with the different "realities" such as financial crises, drugs, disobedient children, brokenness and constant battles, an empowered woman must not allow her emotions to control her but be confident in her strength that comes from God.

You are an instrument of God, created for a purpose – to glorify Him.

When you hear about freedom, you may be tempted to think that you are "free" to say what you want, do what you want and live however you please. This is not so! True liberation for an empowered woman comes when she serves Christ by serving her spouse (if she is married), children and others.

I pray this resource guide challenges you to start seeing yourself, your purpose and how you see others differently, as it did with me. We must get to the place where Christ is our focus and we look to Him and not the world for our affirmation.

I love you. God loves you more!

Crystal Daye

ABOUT THE AUTHOR

I am Crystal Daye, minister, best-selling author of the book "Living A Royal Reality," Entrepreneur, Inspirational Speaker and International Christian Empowerment Coach. As the COO of DayeLight International, a Faith-Based Coaching, and Consultancy Company, I teach women and leaders to monetize their passions and build their brands and businesses using online platforms. It is my desire to see kingdom influencers walk in their calling, increase their influence and passionately pursue purposeful lives, careers, and businesses.

Thank you for purchasing this book! It's been a joy sharing what the Lord placed on my heart. I pray that you will walk in Christ's power and authority to be the empowered woman He has called you to be.

"Be separated from the world"

– 2 Corinthians 6:7

For coaching, speaking and workshop training inquiries, please contact Crystal at info@crystaldaye.com or visit website: www.crystaldaye.com

Connect with me:
Instagram: @crystalsdaye

Made in the USA
Columbia, SC
13 October 2024